What you see here is the Seal of the president of the United States. It's a mighty important symbol. Speaking of important symbols—I'm P.C. I'm a bald eagle. I've been the big bird for the United States almost since the beginning. Would you believe that Benjamin Franklin wanted the turkey to be our national symbol! But that's another story...I'm here to tell you about some famous folks I've known well—presidents of the United States.

In the beginning the United States had no president. Our early leaders were afraid of giving too much power to one person. After all, we'd just spent over ten years fighting to get free from the rule of the king of England.

By 1788 Americans began to realize that somebody had to see that laws were carried out. So the Constitution of the United States established the office of the presidency.

Our Founding Fathers—guys whose names you hear all the time in school: James Madison, Thomas Jefferson, Benjamin Franklin, John Adams, George Washington, and others—intended the office of the president to be more about prestige than power. They'd be real surprised to see how the powers of the presidency have grown over the years.

The United States has had more than 40 presidents. I wish I could say it were different, girls, but so far they've all been men.

So, you ask... how did these men GET to be president? How could I get to be president if I wanted to be? What could I DO if I were president? What interesting things have happened to presidents?

Well...you've asked the right bird. I've been there and seen it all. So here's the straight scoop.

Who can be president? Anyone—if she or he meets certain qualifications. What do you think those qualifications are?

The president must know how to read.

The president must be smart.

The president must have a college degree.

The president cannot have a physical handicap.

Ha, bet I fooled you! None of those things are requirements to be president. The Constitution mentions only a few rules:

The president must be at least 35 years old.

The president must have been born in the United States.

The president must have lived in the United States for 14 years.

No one can become president who has been convicted of a major crime.

That's all there is to it! Well, you do have to get yourself nominated and elected. How? Read on.

This convention business is pretty exciting stuff—I mean, bands, parades, confetti, balloons. The delegates are sure whooping it up for their candidate. Hey—maybe this is why they call them political parties!

Hold it—I think I'm getting ahead of myself. I'd better explain what I'm doing here.

Since the 1860's there have been two main political parties in the United States—the Democratic Party and the Republican Party. People join the party whose ideas about how to run government are most like their own.

Running for president is different from other elected offices. The Democratic and Republican candidates for president are selected at their party's national convention. But before that there may be lots of people interested in being president.

Most states have presidential primaries where voters choose delegates to each party's national convention. When voters choose the delegates, they also vote on the candidate they prefer for president. When the delegates go to the convention, they usually support the candidate who received the most votes in their state's primary election.

In a presidential election year, each party holds its national convention for a week in the summer. Like I said, it's an exciting time—discussions, arguments, speeches. A nominating speech is made for each candidate. After each speech, the supporters of that candidate cheer, blow horns, and march around carrying signs—all while band music plays and balloons are released.

At the end of the week, all the delegates vote for the nominee they prefer. Then the presidential nominee gives an acceptance speech, and there is another big demonstration.

In 1924 the Democrats had to vote 103 times before they selected their nominee for president!

Are you confused yet? Clear as mud, huh? Maybe this diagram will help.

A person decides to become a presidential candidate.

The candidate campaigns in many states, giving speeches and trying to interest people into voting for him or her.

People vote in their state's primary election. They vote for delegates who represent the candidate they like.

The national convention begins.

The convention nominates its candidate for president.

Remember—both political parties have a national convention. So by the end of the summer each party has nominated a candidate for president.

Howdy, pardners! Here we are on the ole campaign trail, tryin' to round-up those votes!

After the party conventions, the presidential campaigns begin. The candidates visit as many states as possible. They stop in large cities and small towns. They visit factories and farms. They give speeches and attend dinners. They kiss babies and shake hands. They are trying to win votes.

In the past, before television brought news to us instantly, traveling around the country by train and bus was about the only way for a candidate to become known by the people.

Nowadays candidates pay lots of money for television "spots" telling how terrific they are—and often how terrific the opponent isn't.

In recent presidential elections, candidates have gone on television together to debate. (In a debate, each person has a certain amount of time to answer a question or say what he/she thinks about an issue.) A debate gives the American people a chance to see how a candidate explains his/her opinions on issues that are important to our country, such as taxes and how government should spend money.

What do you mean I can't graduate from the electoral college?

Every four years, on the first Tuesday after the first Monday in November, Americans go to the polls to select the next president of the United States.

Or do they? What about this thing called the electoral college? What does it have to do with electing the president?

To begin with, the electoral college isn't a school. It's a group of people elected in each state. Their job is to select the president.

You see, when our nation was young, there were dirt roads or no roads, no telephone, no radio, no television. Voters were not familiar with the candidates, so they elected knowledgeable people called electors. The electors met and selected the president. Now days the electoral college is a formality. Most states put the names of the candidates, not the electors, on the ballot.

But it is possible for a candidate to get more votes from the people (called the popular vote) and lose the election. It happened in 1824, 1876, and 1888. Let me explain how that works...

Each state has the same number of electoral votes as it has representatives and senators in the U.S. Congress. Every state has two senators, but the number of representatives is determined by the population of the state. So states with lots of people have lots of votes (like California with 54); states with small populations have few votes (like Wyoming with 3). There are a total of 538 electoral votes. To be elected president requires at least 270 votes.

To win the presidential election, a candidate must win states with large numbers of electoral votes. In the 1992 election, fewer than 6,000,000 popular votes separated the winner, Bill Clinton, from the loser, George Bush. But the electoral vote wasn't even close. Clinton had 370 votes; Bush 168. Clinton won the "big" states of California, New York, Pennsylvania, Ohio, Illinois, and Michigan.

The electors meet on the first Monday after the second Wednesday in December. They gather in their state and vote for their party's candidates. Certified, sealed lists of their votes are mailed to the president of the U.S. Senate. He/she opens them in a joint session of Congress on January 6.

So how is it we know on the night of the election in November who the next president will be? I thought you might ask that question, so I was ready for it:

The Constitution does not require the electors to vote for the candidate who won the popular vote in their state. But in fact, they do. The election results aren't truly official, though, until those electoral votes are counted on January 6.

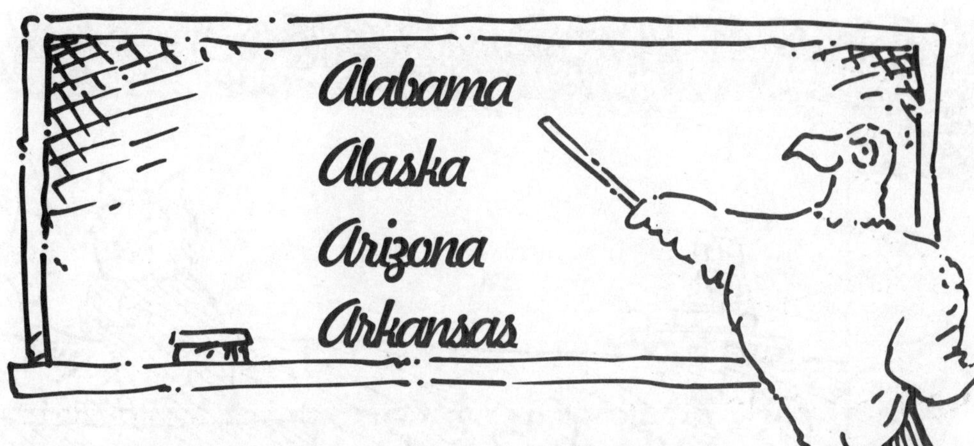

Even though this electoral college stuff is a little confusing, it's pretty interesting. See if you can figure out the minimum number of states it would take to get the 270 vote majority needed to be president. Which ones are they?

State	Votes	State	Votes	State	Votes
Alabama	9	Kentucky	8	North Dakota	3
Alaska	3	Louisiana	9	Ohio	21
Arizona	8	Maine	4	Oklahoma	8
Arkansas	6	Maryland	10	Oregon	7
California	54	Massachusetts	12	Pennsylvania	23
Colorado	8	Michigan	18	Rhode Island	4
Connecticut	8	Minnesota	10	South Carolina	8
Delaware	3	Mississippi	7	South Dakota	3
District of Columbia	3	Missouri	11	Tennessee	11
Florida	25	Montana	3	Texas	32
Georgia	13	Nebraska	5	Utah	5
Hawaii	4	Nevada	4	Vermont	3
Idaho	4	New Hampshire	4	Virginia	13
Illinois	22	New Jersey	15	Washington	11
Indiana	12	New Mexico	5	West Virginia	5
Iowa	7	New York	33	Wisconsin	11
Kansas	6	North Carolina	14	Wyoming	3

January 20 is Inauguration Day. It's the big day for the president-elect.

Up till this day, the president-elect has been working closely with the outgoing president to learn everything that's happening. A lot of these things are top secret.

The new president is inaugurated at noon on the eastern steps of the Capitol Building. The Chief Justice of the Supreme Court swears in the new president. The new president places his/her left hand of the Bible, raises his/her right hand slightly and repeats the presidential oath of office.

> "I do solemnly swear (or affirm) that I will faithfully execute the office of president of the United States, and will, to the best of my ability, preserve, protect, and defend the Constitution of the United States."

The Constitution said that the president will serve for a four-year term, but it did not mention how many times a president could be reelected.

For almost 150 years, no president had served more than two terms. In fact it became a matter of tradition, until Franklin Roosevelt was elected to a third term in 1940, and then a fourth term in 1944.

This worried some Americans. They believed it gave a president too much power to serve so long. In 1951 the 22nd Amendment became a part of the Constitution. It limits the president to two consecutive terms.

Facts About the Presidency

Term: 4 years

Salary: $200,000 a year. Plus $100,000 travel allowance, $50,000 for expenses, and $20,000 for official entertainment.

Successor: If the president dies or is removed from office, he/she is succeeded by the vice-president, followed by the Speaker of the House and the president pro tempore (for the time being) of the Senate.

How Removed: Impeachment. This means to be bring charges against for wrongdoing. The House of Representatives impeaches a president. The Senate conducts the trial. Only one president, Andrew Johnson, was impeached. But the Senate was one vote short of a conviction, so Johnson remained in office.

One president has resigned the presidency. That was Richard M. Nixon in 1974. Many think that he would have been impeached and removed from office had he not resigned.

The president of the United States is one of the most powerful people in the world. The Constitution gives the president several kinds of powers.

Executive Powers

- Makes appointments to the executive branch
- Sees that federal laws are carried out
- Supervises all federal agencies

Legislative Powers

- Suggests laws to Congress
- Signs or vetoes laws (but Congress can override a veto)
- Calls Congress into special session
- Sends special messages to Congress

Judicial Powers

- Appoints federal and Supreme Court Justices (but the Senate must approve)
- Grants pardons and reprieves (can set a prisoner free or postpone punishment)

Military Powers

- Is the Commander-in-Chief of the armed forces
- Can send armed forces anywhere in the world

Diplomatic Powers

- Makes treaties (must be approved by the Senate)
- Appoints ambassadors to other countries
- Makes agreements with other countries

You can see that even though the president of the United States has a lot of power, Congress can overrule many things the president may do. This goes back to the "Founding Fathers'" notion that too much power by one person or part of the government is dangerous. This is called balance of power or checks and balances.

I'm perched at one of the most famous addresses in the world—1600 Pennsylvania Avenue, Washington, D.C. It's called the White House, the residence of the president. Every president has lived here—that is, except George Washington—that's because it wasn't built yet.

White House History

George Washington picked the location for the president's residence. A man named James Hoban won $500 for his design.

Construction was started in 1792, but it wasn't yet finished in 1800 when John Adams, our second president moved in. The building was called the president's Palace, not the White House, <u>and</u> it was gray.

In 1814 the U.S. was at war with England again. The British burned the White House, but Dolley Madison, wife of president James Madison, saved a famous painting of George Washington by artist Gilbert Stuart.

During president Truman's term, the floors were found to be unsafe. He and Mrs. Truman moved out from 1949-1951 while the inside of the building was rebuilt.

Jacqueline Kennedy, wife of president John F. Kennedy, did much redecorating of the White House between 1961 and 1963.

I never miss a chance to visit the White House when I'm in Washington. Of course, I'm always in demand as a guest at official functions.

White House Facts

- The White House sits on 18 beautifully landscaped acres in the heart of Washington, D.C.
- The White House has 132 rooms spread out over six floors, two of which are underground.
- Certain rooms on the ground and state floor are open to the public. Over 1,000,000 tourists visit the White House each year.
- The president and his family have private rooms on the two floors about the state floor.
- The White House has a bowling alley, an indoor swimming pool, and a movie theater for the president's family to use.
- The president's office—the Oval Office—is located in the west wing of the White House.
- Teddy Roosevelt let his children ride their pony in the East Room!

Here is a map of the ground and state floors of the White House. You don't have to be a birdbrain like me to figure out the colors used in the decor of some rooms!

This is a working library for White House staff.

Ground Floor

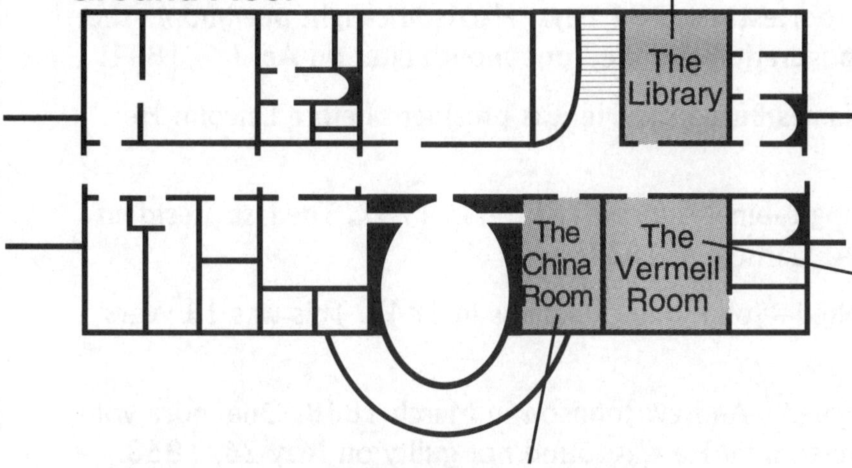

The Library

The China Room

The Vermeil Room

Holds a collection of vermeil (gold-covered silver) given to the White House in 1956. The room is used as a sitting room during formal occasions.

Displays pieces of china, glassware, and silverware used by almost every past president.

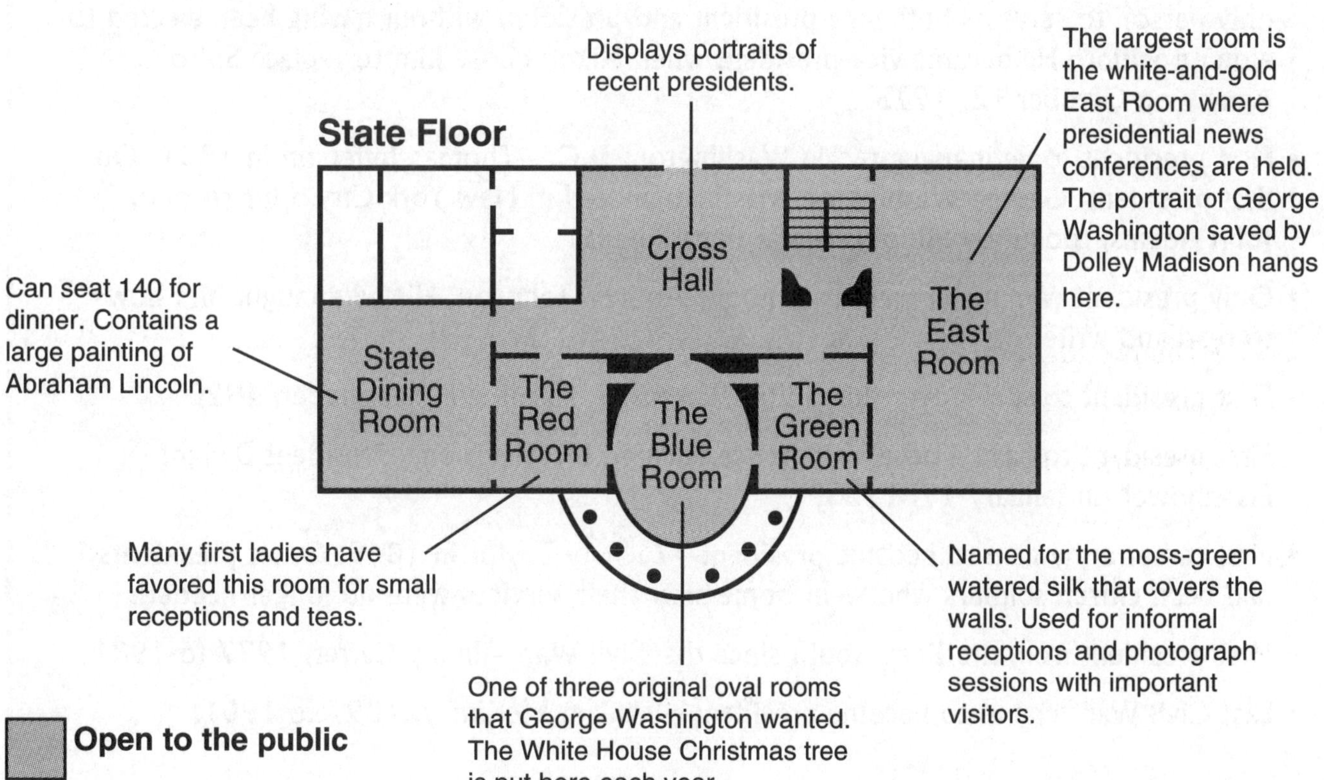

Open to the public

Presidential Firsts

OK, troops. Now you know almost as much as I do about being president. But I've got a lot more great information under my wing—like these presidential Firsts.

- First president to die in office — William Henry Harrison. He also served the shortest term: 31 days. Harrison caught pneumonia shortly after his inauguration and died one month later on April 4, 1841.
- Our only bachelor president—James Buchanan. He was president before Lincoln. He served from 1857 to 1861.
- First president to be born in a log cabin—Andrew Jackson in 1767. The last president born in a log cabin was James A. Garfield in 1831.
- First president to be photographed—John Quincy Adams in 1847. This was 18 years after he left the White House.
- The only president to be impeached—Andrew Johnson in March 1868. One more vote in the Senate would have convicted him. He was found not guilty on May 26, 1868.
- The only president to resign—Richard M. Nixon on August 9, 1974. He was succeeded by vice-president Gerald Ford. Ford also deserves a place in presidential firsts. He is the only person to serve as both vice-president and president without having been elected to either position. He became vice-president when Nixon chose him to replace Spiro Agnew on October 12, 1973.
- First president to be inaugurated in Washington, D.C.—Thomas Jefferson in 1801. Our first president, George Washington, was inaugurated in New York City. Our second, John Adams, took the oath of office in Philadelphia.
- Only president who never went to school—Andrew Johnson. His wife taught him how to read and write.
- First president to speak over the radio—Warren G. Harding in September, 1920.
- First president to have a news conference covered by television—President Dwight D. Eisenhower on January 19, 1955.
- First career army man to become president—Zachary Taylor in 1849. Other presidents had been citizen soldiers who went home after their services were no longer needed.
- First president from the Deep South since the Civil War—Jimmy Carter, 1977 to 1981.
- Last Civil War veteran to become president—William McKinley, 1897 to 1901.

Word Search

Find the "firsts" and circle them on the word search. They run horizontally, vertically, and diagonally.

U S F S D R D O E L K S S W H C R

N O L U H A R D I N G M W A O E P

C I H J T S W F C I A I T D W Z I

P D S F O R D C V D R A O O M A A

L Z K W W H G L A P F D H F M W I

Z B U C H A N A N D I N R G R R L

J D O C A R S S N X E E L H E O Q

L A O C R Y R H O S L O O P V N J

E R C Q R O J Y I N D J I O Q L B

O M C K I N L E Y N F I F A L D N

V U A U S W S J F L G H H H Q J D

O X R N O O M V E F F T U P B W H

S Y T L N G N Y J V E R O C C K Q

D F E R Y X I K Y M L R X N Q I N

C U R P E I A N I X O N S L K V M

Z Q W Z S D I C F L C P H O G L A

Z Z F H E V W U Y Q L K F O N N A

Z T Y X L M W A T G A M P B W U Z

W I T C R O T B B U U M Q E C C M

Word Box

ADAMS	GARFIELD	JEFFERSON
BUCHANAN	HARDING	MCKINLEY
CARTER	HARRISON	NIXON
EISENHOWER	JACKSON	TAYLOR
FORD	JOHNSON	WASHINGTON

Did you know that...

I tell ya, in over 200 years I've learned a bunch of stuff! Did you know that...

- Eight presidents have died in office. They are William Henry Harrison, Zachary Taylor, Abraham Lincoln, James Garfield, William McKinley, Warren G. Harding, Franklin D. Roosevelt, and John F. Kennedy.
- Four presidents have been assassinated. They are Lincoln, Garfield, McKinley, and Kennedy.
- Three presidents died on the 4th of July. Both Thomas Jefferson and John Adams in 1826; James Monroe in 1831.
- The president who served the longest term was Franklin D. Roosevelt. He was president from 1933 to 1945. He was elected four times. He died several months into his fourth term.
- The president with the most children was John Tyler. He had 14. Second was William Henry Harrison with 10. Six presidents had no children. They were Washington, Madison, Jackson, Polk, Wilson, and Harding.
- Our smallest president was James Madison. He stood 5' 4" tall and weighed 100 pounds. The tallest president was Abraham Lincoln at 6' 4". The heaviest was William Howard Taft at 326 pounds!
- The youngest president when inaugurated was Theodore Roosevelt. He was 42. John F. Kennedy was 43. Ronald Reagan was the oldest at 69.
- One president occupied the White House on separate occasions. Grover Cleveland was president from 1885 to 1889 and again from 1893 to 1897.
- Only one father and son have been presidents—John Adams (1797-1801) and John Quincy Adams (1825-1829). Benjamin Harrison (1889-1893) was the grandson of William Henry Harrison (March-April 1841).
- Teddy Roosevelt was quite a hunter, but once refused to shoot a bear cub. News of this inspired a cartoon which in turn inspired a toy manufacturer to create—you guessed it—the Teddy Bear.

Because they were famous, we get to know lots of interesting (and silly) things about presidents.

- John Quincy Adams, president from 1825 to 1829, enjoyed early morning swims in the Potomac River. He went alone—in those days presidents didn't always have someone guarding them. One morning, while he was taking his refreshing swim, someone stole his clothes from the river bank. The embarrassed and nude president convinced a boy who was passing by to run to the White House and get him a new set of clothing.
- Abraham Lincoln, president from 1861 to 1865, liked to tell about an incident that occurred years before he became president. One day while out horseback riding, Lincoln met a woman at a cross-roads. The woman looked up at Lincoln and said, "Sir, I do believe you are the ugliest man I have ever seen!" Lincoln, taken by surprise, defended himself by saying, "But, madam, I can't help how I look." "That's true," replied the woman. "But at least you could stay indoors!"
- Benjamin Harrison, president from 1889 to 1893, was afraid of electric lights. Electricity was installed in the White House during Harrison's term. He and his wife never turned on the lights in their bedroom for fear of being electrocuted. Hall lights and lights in other parts of the executive mansion were left on all night. Harrison waited for the White House electrician to arrive each morning and turn off the lights.
- Andrew Jackson was the first president not descended from a wealthy family. As a "man of the people," he invited the public to a White House reception following his inauguration. More than 20,000 showed up and turned it into a riot. Refreshments included a 1,400-pound cheese which was trampled into rugs and furniture—the odor remained for months.
- William Howard Taft was so large that he got stuck in the White House bathtub and had to be rescued. A special tub, big enough for four men, was built for him.
- Theodore Roosevelt had five rambunctious children. Quentin organized his classmates and dropped a giant snowball off a White House balcony onto a policeman. Ethel loved to "toboggan" down the White House stairs on a cookie sheet. Alice was also a great mischief maker. About her behavior Roosevelt said, "I can run the country or control Alice, but not both."

Presidents are just about my favorite subject. I could go on and on and on. But, hey, they've only given me 32 pages, so I'd better cut to the chase. Let me tell you a bit about a few of notable presidents. Let's start with the Father of Our Country. You guessed it, old GW himself.

George Washington

George Washington was a true American hero. When a young nation needed leadership during the Revolutionary War, it was Washington who stepped forward. When his country needed him to serve as its first president, he was ready. Duty to country came first to this patriotic American from Virginia.

Few people gave America any chance of victory in its War for Independence against Great Britain. A ragged colonial army was matched against one of the most powerful armies in Europe. Great Britain also had the strongest navy in the world. How, then, did America win?

The answer lies with George Washington. As general of the colonial army, he was a brilliant military planner and a strict disciplinarian. He turned the ragtag colonial army into a strong fighting force. Although he was strict, his troops loved and respected him. Together they endured many hardships. Spurred on by Washington's courage and leadership, the American army won the war and helped create a new nation.

For the first eight years of its independence, the United States did not have a president. By 1787, the need for a chief executive was apparent. The Constitutional Convention met at Philadelphia in 1787. It ended up writing a new plan of government, the Constitution. George Washington was chosen as chairman of that convention. His efforts helped convince the 13 new states to ratify, or accept, the new Constitution.

Washington returned to his home in Virginia. He hoped to live out his days as a planter. But his country needed him once more. He received notice on April 14, 1789, that he had been chosen as president. He went on to serve his country for two terms. Under his guidance, a young nation grew and prospered.

UpCloseandPersonal

It was hard not to notice George Washington as he walked by. He stood 6′ 2″ tall and weighed 200 pounds. He had broad shoulders and powerful hands. He also had very large feet. He wore a size 13 shoe, a real oddity in those days. His handsome appearance was marred only by smallpox scars on his face.

If paintings picture Washington as tight-lipped and sad-looking, there was a reason for this. His artificial teeth fit badly and bothered him throughout his life. You probably wouldn't smile for a picture either, if your false teeth hurt—especially if they were made of wood, as were Washington's!

You have probably heard the story of how Washington as a boy chopped down his father's cherry tree. He supposedly confessed to his father, saying that he could not tell a lie. The story is not true. It was invented by an early author to make Washington appear to be as perfect and faultless as possible.

George Washington was not perfect. He had faults like everyone else. But no one can deny that he was a great American.

The letters in the circles spell out the name of Washington's Virginia plantation—now a national monument.

Citizen of the U.S.

War for Independence

State where Washington lived

Washington was the first

Tree he supposedly chopped

Washington was a ____ in the army

A person in the army

Washington's teeth were ____

Thomas Jefferson

Talk about talent, our third president had it all!

Diplomat, writer, architect, inventor, philosopher, violinist, lawyer—Thomas Jefferson was all of these things—and more. He did so many things well. He was without doubt one of the most talented Americans ever to occupy the White House.

Thomas Jefferson was the third president of the United states. He served two terms, from 1801 to 1809.

Jefferson was 58 when he became president. But his place in history had been guaranteed 25 years earlier. In 1776, at the age of 33, he wrote our country's Declaration of Independence from Great Britain. He considered it his most important achievement.

A major event of Jefferson's presidency was the Louisiana Purchase. In 1803, our government paid France $15 million for what was called the Louisiana Territory. It consisted of 825,000 acres between the Mississippi River and the Rocky Mountains. Part or all of 15 states were later created from this vast area. Its purchase doubled the size of the United States.

It is interesting that Jefferson did not consider the Louisiana Purchase a major accomplishment. Nor the fact that he had been both a president and a vice-president. Nor that he had once been the governor of Virginia and our country's ambassador to France.

Of what was Thomas Jefferson the most proud? Three things are mentioned on his tombstone, which he designed himself before his death. First was the Declaration of Independence. Next was the Statute of Religious Freedom for the State of Virginia. This was a law granting freedom of worship in his home state. Jefferson got it passed while serving as a representative in the Virginia legislature. The last achievement mentioned on Jefferson's tombstone is the University of Virginia. Jefferson founded it and designed its buildings. He even hired its first teachers. The university fulfilled one of his lifelong dreams.

Thomas Jefferson, like George Washington, was a homebody at heart. When governmental duties did not call him away, he loved working and doing things at Monticello, his home in Virginia.

Jefferson is credited with a number of inventions. Among these were a copying machine, a dumbwaiter elevator, and an improved plow. Others included the swivel chair and a movable bed on pulleys.

He also had an interest in archaeology. He kept a large collection of fossil bones at the White House that he had found and dug up himself.

Jefferson was a very well educated. He could speak and write five languages. He also played the violin. The large collection of books he accumulated over his lifetime became the basis for the U.S. Library of Congress.

Thomas Jefferson was a loving family man. He never completely recovered from the unexpected death of his young wife, Martha, in 1782. As she lay on her death bed, he promised her he would never remarry. He never did. He devoted the remainder of his life to his daughters, Martha and Mary.

Here is a part of one of the most famous documents in history, the Declaration of Independence, written by Thomas Jefferson and adopted by the Continental Congress in Philadelphia, July 4, 1776.

> We hold these Truths to be self-evident, that all Men are created equal, that they are endowed by their Creator with certain unalienable Rights, that among these are Life, Liberty and the Pursuit of Happiness...

What do you think these words mean? Do you think people in the United States today have these rights?

Abraham Lincoln

I really liked old Abe. He was about as down-home as they come. He was also a man of great courage who stood firm for his beliefs.

Few presidents have entered the White House during more troubled times than Abraham Lincoln. Before he had even taken the oath of office, seven southern states had withdrawn from the Union. And one month after his inauguration, the Civil War began.

Lincoln had gained national recognition earlier from a series of debates with Stephen A. Douglas. In 1858, Lincoln was running for a Senate seat against Douglas. Douglas won the election but most people thought that Lincoln had come out on top in the debates. The debates centered around the spread of slavery into Kansas and Nebraska. These were not states then, but territories. Douglas favored letting the two territories decide whether they would permit slavery. Lincoln was against the further spread of slavery anywhere. A nation separated into slave and free states troubled Lincoln. "A house divided against itself cannot stand," he pointed out during the debates.

Abraham Lincoln held this same view when the Civil War began in 1861. He made enemies when he stated that the Union must be saved, whatever the cost. There were people in the North who favored letting the South break away. In their opinion, it was not worth a war to force them to stay in. Even some of the president's Cabinet members supported taking no action against the South.

Lincoln showed even greater courage when he emancipated (freed) all the slaves in the states at war against the Union. He did this through the Emancipation Proclamation in 1863. When the Union won the war in 1865, there were those who wanted revenge against the president because of his actions. On April 14, 1865, he was assassinated by John Wilkes Booth, an actor who had been a southern sympathizer. With one shot from a small pistol, Booth took a great leader away from the American people.

Abraham Lincoln, at 6' 4", was our tallest president. His 180 pounds were spread out over a lean frame. Yet he was a very strong person. He could out-run and out-wrestle any man in southwestern Indiana, where he spent his teen years. He was also a champion at rail-splitting and lifting heavy barrels.

Lincoln had many nicknames during his lifetime. He was once known as the Rail Splitter because he was so good with an ax. As president, he became known as the Great Emancipator for freeing the slaves. He is best known as Honest Abe. He got this name when, he was a young storekeeper. One day he accidentally shortchanged a customer six cents. Legend has it that he walked two miles to return the person's money.

Across

2. He shot Lincoln.
3. To quit or break away
6. _____ Proclamation
9. _____ War
10. "_____ Splitter"
11. What Lincoln said must be saved.

Down

1. "_____ Abe"
4. Number of southern states to secede before Lincoln's inauguration.
5. Lincoln debated him.
7. _____ Lincoln
8. Lincoln lived here as a teenager.

Woodrow Wilson

Here's another president who served during a difficult time in our history.

Woodrow Wilson was the twenty-eighth president of the United States. He served from 1913 to 1921. During his second term, he guided America through the First World War and the troubled peace that followed. The stress brought on by these events severely affected his health. Eventually it helped lead to his death.

After America helped defeat Germany and it's allies, Wilson was hopeful of a lasting peace. He wrote a plan called the Fourteen Points. The plan called for the defeated nations to be treated fairly. But France, England and other countries wanted to make Germany pay for starting the war. They also wanted to keep territories they had gained during the fighting. They had no interest in Wilson's ideas for a fair peace.

Another part of the Fourteen Points was the League of Nations. This was an organization set up to prevent wars in the future. This part of Wilson's plan was accepted. But although 63 nations joined the League, the United States did not. The U.S. Senate rejected, or voted against, it. The Senate's action was a severe blow to the president.

Before the Senate vote, Wilson went on a cross-country tour. He had hoped to win support for the League. He visited many cities in a short of length of time. The pace was hectic. At Pueblo, Colorado, he suffered a stroke. News of the Senate vote made his health even worse. He became an invalid and remained so until his death in 1924.

The League of Nations proved unsuccessful in keeping the peace. It had no way of making other nations follow its decisions. During the 1930's, Germany, Italy, and Japan ignored the League altogether. Their military actions helped bring on World War II.

Woodrow Wilson was an extremely intelligent man. He taught at Princeton University and for 12 years was the university's president. He was a respected historian whose books were used as texts in schools.

Many people disliked Wilson. They saw him as uncaring, impatient, and snobbish. Wilson did have another side. He was a devoted husband and the loving father of three daughters. His favorite form of entertainment was vaudeville, an often-silly kind of stage show with singers, dancers, comedians, and animal acts.

In 1945, 21 years after Woodrow Wilson's death, a new international organization was formed with the goal of maintaining world peace. It remains active today, with a membership of 184 nations.

Decipher the code to find the name of this organization.

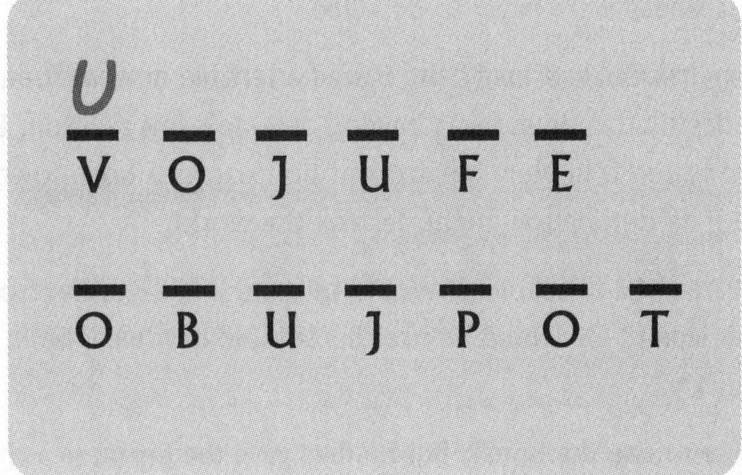

Harry S. Truman

Every president in our history has had to make difficult decisions. But none had to make a more difficult decision than president Harry S. Truman in 1945.

World War II had dragged on for six long years. Millions of people had been killed. Millions more were wounded or missing. When would it all end?

Nazi Germany had surrendered in May, 1945. That left Japan. But Japan showed no signs of giving up. Although they were losing the war, the Japanese continued to fight. The leaders of our military knew that Japan itself would have to be invaded for the war to end. It was estimated that a half million Americans would die in an invasion of the Japanese islands. Twice that many Japanese were likely to be killed.

By 1945, the United States had made and tested a terrible new weapon. It was the atomic bomb. Its destructive power was beyond anyone's imagination. Even the scientists who built and tested it in New Mexico had no clear idea how powerful it really was. Several wondered if its detonation might destroy the world.

President Truman weighed his choices. Would he send a half million troops to their deaths by invading Japan? Or would he use this terrible new weapon in the hope of ending the war quickly?

The president chose to use the bomb. But he first gave the Japanese a chance to surrender. American planes dropped leaflets over Japanese cities. The leaflets warned the Japanese that America had a new weapon capable of causing mass destruction. Japan was asked to surrender. Its leaders refused.

On August 6, 1945, the first atomic bomb was dropped on the city of Hiroshima. Even though 78,000 people were killed, Japan still refused to quit fighting. Three days later, a second bomb was dropped on Nagasaki. It killed 74,000. This time, the Japanese surrendered. World War II was over.

Many people criticized president Truman for using the bomb. And the United States was condemned for being the only nation in history to use an atomic bomb in warfare. This criticism continues today.

Did you know that the "S" in president Truman's name stood for nothing? His middle name was simply "S".

Both of Truman's grandfathers had last names beginning with "S". One was named Shippe and the other Solomon. His mother did not want to offend either by naming her son after the other. So she used the "S" to stand for both last names.

Truman was known for being a man of strong convictions. He was an early advocate of increased rights and opportunities for Black Americans. Despite opposition from other Democrats, he did not change his position.

A sign on Truman's desk read, "The Buck Stops Here." This meant he knew that as president he was responsible for major decisions—that he could not put the blame on anyone else.

What do you think?

- Was president Truman right to use the atomic bomb against Japan? ______________________________

____

____

- What would you have done had you been president?

____

____

____

Talk about this with someone.

More Presidential Portraits

Can you name each of these presidents?

I was the main writer of the Constitution and the Bill of Rights.

I was the fourth president, serving from 1809 to 1817.

I was living in the White House when the British burned it during the War of 1812.

I was president from 1901 to 1909.

I became a national hero when I lead the Rough Riders during the Spanish-American War.

I negotiated the agreement to build the Panama Canal.

I was elected to a record four terms of office.

During my presidency (1933 - 1945), the U.S. went through the Great Depression and World War II.

I had polio as an adult and needed crutches or a wheelchair to get around.

As supreme commander of the Allied forces in Europe during World War II, I helped plan the D-Day invasion of Normandy in 1944.

I was elected president two times—in 1952 and 1956.

My nickname was Ike.

I was elected president in 1960.

As president, I founded the Peace Corps, supported racial integration in the South, and ordered the Soviet Union to remove missiles from Cuba.

I was assassinated in 1963 while visiting Dallas, Texas.

As John Kennedy's vice-president, I became president after his death and was re-elected in 1964.

I worked hard to pass civil rights laws and called for a war on poverty.

Many people disagreed with my decisions to increase U.S. involvement in the war in Vietnam.

I was president from 1969 to 1974.

I made an historic visit to the People's Republic of China.

I resigned from office after being accused of authorizing and covering up a break-in at the headquarters of the Democratic Party.

When president Nixon resigned in 1974, I became president.

I exercised a presidential power and granted Nixon a pardon.

The Vietnam War finally came to an end while I was president.

I ran for reelection in 1976 but lost to Jimmy Carter.

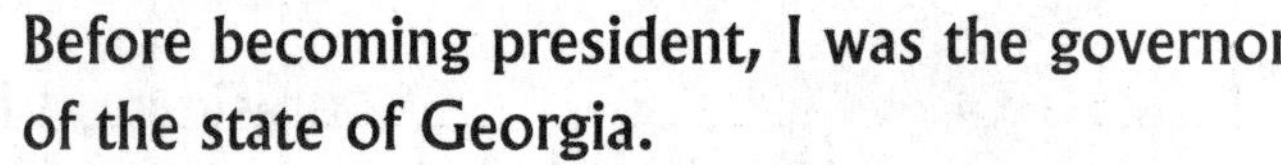

Before becoming president, I was the governor of the state of Georgia.

I worked hard to create jobs and reduce unemployment.

After leaving the presidency in 1981, I helped negotiate a peace agreement between Egypt and Isreal.

Before becoming president, I had been a movie actor and later the governor of California.

As president, I held an important meeting with the leader of the Soviet Union, Mikhail Gobachev. This lead to reductions in nuclear weapons.

During World War II, I was the youngest pilot in the U.S. Navy.

I was Ronald Reagan's vice-president and then ran for president in 1988.

In 1990, I sent U.S. troops to the Persian Gulf to repel Iraq's invasion of Kuwait.

I lost the 1992 presidential election to Bill Clinton.

I served as governor of Arkansas for five terms.

I was elected president in 1992.

I have tried to reform health care in the United States.

I favored the North American Free Trade Agreement which makes it easier for the U.S., Mexico, and Canada to buy and sell each other's products.

Presidential Crossword

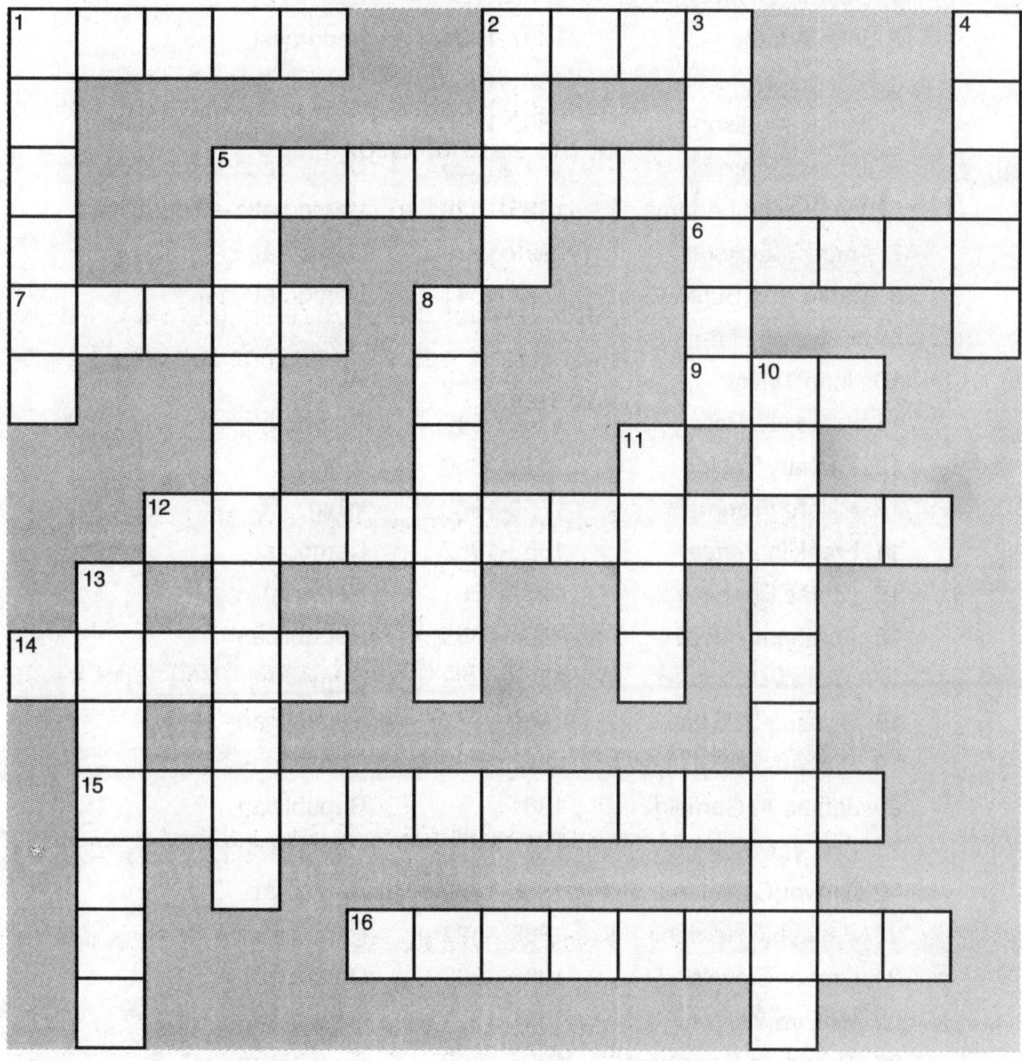

Across

1. Washington was the ____ U.S. president.
2. Presidents swear an ____ when they are inaugurated.
5. Candidates _______ for votes.
6. We ____ presidents in the United States
7. A presidential inauguration is an important one.
9. A president can only be elected for ___ terms.
12. Swearing-in ceremony for a new president
14. The war between the north and south: ______ War
15. The basic laws of the United States are found in it.
16. Thomas ______ wrote the Declaration of Independence.

Down

1. Washington was called the _______ of his country.
2. The president's office in the White House: _______ Office
3. Lincoln's nickname: _______ Abe
4. Washington had wooden false _________.
5. Candidates are selected at presidential _________.
8. Pres. Wilson tried to establish a _______ of Nations.
10. The residence of the president
11. The largest room in the White House: _____ Room
13. The president who emancipated the slaves

WordBank

campaign	east	first	league	teeth
civil	elect	honest	Lincoln	two
constitution	event	inauguration	oath	White House
conventions	father	Jefferson	oval	

UNITED STATES PRESIDENTS

1. George Washington	1789-1797	Federalist
2. John Adams	1797-1801	Federalist
3.Thomas Jefferson	1801-1809	Democratic—Republican
4. James Madison	1809-1817	Democratic—Republican
5. James Monroe	1817-1825	Democratic—Republican
6. John Quincy Adams	1825-1829	Democratic—Republican
7. Andrew Jackson	1829-1837	Democrat
8. Martin Van Buren	1837-1841	Democrat
9. William H. Harrison	1841	Whig
10. John Tyler	1841-1845	Whig
11. James K. Polk	1845-1849	Democrat
12. Zachary Taylor	1849-1850	Whig
13. Millard Fillmore	1850-1853	Whig
14. Franklin Pierce	1853-1857	Democrat
15. James Buchanan	1857-1861	Democrat
16. Abraham Lincoln	1861-1865	Republican
17. Andrew Johnson	1866-1869	Democrat
18. Ulysses S. Grant	1869-1877	Republican
19. Rutherford B. Hayes	1877-1881	Republican
20. James A. Garfield	1881	Republican
21. Chester A. Arthur	1881-1885	Republican
22. Grover Cleveland	1885-1889	Democrat
23. Benjamin Harrison	1889-1893	Republican
24. Grover Cleveland	1893-1897	Democrat
25. William McKinley	1897-1901	Republican
26. Theodore Roosevelt	1901-1909	Republican
27. William Howard Taft	1909-1913	Republican
28. Woodrow Wilson	1913-1921	Democrat
29. Warren G. Harding	1921-1923	Republican
30. Calvin Coolidge	1923-1929	Republican
31. Herbert C. Hoover	1929-1933	Republican
32. Franklin D. Roosevelt	1933-1945	Democrat
33. Harry S. Truman	1945-1953	Democrat
34. Dwight D. Eisenhower	1953-1961	Republican
35. John F. Kennedy	1961-1963	Democrat
36. Lyndon B. Johnson	1963-1969	Democrat
37. Richard M. Nixon	1969-1974	Republican
38. Gerald R. Ford	1974-1977	Republican
39. James Earl Carter	1977-1981	Democrat
40. Ronald W. Reagan	1981-1989	Republican
41. George Bush	1989-1993	Republican
42. Bill Clinton	1993-	Democrat